Court Franco-Siamese Mixed

The Case of Kieng Chek Kham Muon

Before the Franco-Siamese Mixed Court. Constitution of the Mixed Court

Court Franco-Siamese Mixed

The Case of Kieng Chek Kham Muon
Before the Franco-Siamese Mixed Court. Constitution of the Mixed Court

ISBN/EAN: 9783337157951

Printed in Europe, USA, Canada, Australia, Japan

Cover: Foto ©Suzi / pixelio.de

More available books at **www.hansebooks.com**

Kingdom of Siam.

The Case of Kieng Chek (Kham Muon)

BEFORE THE

FRANCO-SIAMESE MIXED COURT.

CONSTITUTION OF THE MIXED COURT.

AND

RULES OF PROCEDURE.

THE TRIAL, JUDGMENT AND CONDEMNATION OF PHRA YOT.

JUNE 1894.

𝔉𝔯𝔞𝔫𝔠𝔬=𝔖𝔦𝔞𝔪𝔢𝔰𝔢 𝔐𝔦𝔵𝔢𝔡 ℭ𝔬𝔲𝔯𝔱.

AFFAIR OF KHAM MUON (KIENG CHEK).

FIRST PART.

Constitution of the Mixed Court.—Rules of Procedure.

On the 20th of March 1894, the Minister Resident of the French Republic at Bangkok informed the Siamese Minister for Foreign Affairs that the French Government had decided to submit the Judgment given by the Siamese Court, on the 17th March, 1894, to a Mixed Court, according to the right given it by the Convention of 3rd October, 1893. (1).

On the 2nd April, following, M. Jos. Pilinski, Chargé d'Affaires of the French Republic, notified to H. R. H. Prince Devawongse that the French Government had decided the composition of that Court, which would be composed of a President assisted by two Siamese Judges and two French Judges. In the same letter, M. Pilinski gave the names of the Judges appointed by the French Government, (2) and requested H. R. H. Prince Devawongse to inform him of the names of the Siamese Judges appointed by the Government of His Majesty.

The 6th April, H. R. H. Prince Devawongse answered giving the names of the two judges appointed by the Siamese Government, and requesting to be informed of the intention of the French Government concerning the rules to be followed by the Mixed Court in the proceedings and judgment of the case.

In answer to this request, the French Chargé d'Affaires forwarded, on the 18th May following, to the Minister of Foreign Affairs in Bangkok, the text of Rules of Procedure to which some slight alterations were made by mutual consent and which were finally adopted on the 26th May.

These Rules are the following :

Rules of Procedure to be followed before the Franco-Siamese Mixed Court

appointed to judge the Phra Yot Affair.

1. Three days at least before the opening of the sittings, the Act of Accusation drawn up by the Public Prosecutor shall be notified to the Accused.

2. The Court shall sit on the day and at the hour appointed by the President for the opening of the sittings, in a room of the French legation.

3. The Judges, the Witnesses, and the Accused not speaking the same language, the President shall appoint interpreters who shall be duly sworn to translate faithfully the words to be conveyed to those who speak different languages.

4. The Accused, assisted by his Counsel, shall appear free and only accompanied by guards to prevent him from escaping. The President shall ask him his name, age, profession and the place of his birth, then shall warn him to be attentive to what he is about to hear. Immediately after, the President shall order the Recorder to read the Act of Accusation. The Recorder shall read it aloud.

(1.) Convention of 3rd October, 1893, Art. III. "The authors of the outrages of Tong Kieng "Kham and Kham Muon shall be tried by the Siamese authorities ; a Representative of France "shall be present at the trial, and watch the execution of the penalties pronounced. The "French Government reserves to itself the right of appreciating if the condemnations are sufficient, "and, eventually to claim a new trial before a Mixed Court, whereof it shall determine the "composition."

(2.) President : M. Mondot, President of the Court of Appeal of Hanoi ; Judges : M. Camatte, Counsellor of the Court of Appeal of Saigon, and Fuynel, Procureur de la République at Mytho; Public Prosecutor : M. Durwell, Procureur de la République at Saigon.

5. The Public Prosecutor shall lay before the Court the grounds of the Accusation and shall afterwards give a list of the witnesses called both by himself and by the accused.

This list shall be read aloud by the Recorder.

6. The President shall order the witnesses to withdraw to a room prepared for them. They shall not leave this room except to give their evidence.

7. The Accused shall be examined, then the witnesses shall be heard, after having been sworn before this Court to say all the truth and nothing but the truth; the Recorder shall note this as well as their names, professions and residence.

8. After the evidence of each witness, the President shall ask the Accused if he wishes to answer to what has just been said against him.

It shall not be allowed to interrupt the witness; the accused or his counsel shall be allowed to put him questions through the President, after he shall have given his evidence, and to lay before the Court anything against the witness or his evidence that might be useful to the defence of the Accused.

The President shall also have the right to ask from the witness or the accused any explanation he shall deem necessary to discover the truth.

The Judges and the Public Prosecutor shall have the same facility after they have asked the President's leave.

9. During the whole course of the trial, the President shall have the right to hear all witnesses and to obtain all information which he shall deem necessary to discover the truth.

10. After the hearing of the witnesses and the observations to which their evidence may have given rise, the Public Prosecutor shall be heard, and shall develop before the Court the circumstances upon which the accusation is based.

The Accused and his Counsel shall have the right to answer.

The Public Prosecutor shall be allowed to reply but the accused or his Counsel shall always have the right to speak last.

The President shall then declare the debates closed.

11. The President shall put the questions arising from the debates in these words: "Is the accused guilty of having committed such a deed, with all the circumstances contained in the Act of Accusation." Then he shall put the question of extenuating circumstances.

12. After the questions shall have been read by the President, the Accused, his Counsel, and the Public Prosecutor shall be allowed to make any observations, on the way the questions are put, which they will deem fit. If the Public Prosecutor or the Accused object to the way in which a question is put, the Court shall decide on the merits of their objection.

13. The President shall then order the Accused to retire, and the Court shall withdraw to the Chamber of deliberation to deliberate upon the solution of the questions and the punishment to be awarded.

In case of Condemnation the punishment shall be inflicted according to the following rules, viz:

Art. 1.—Homicide committed voluntarily is called murder.

Art. 2.—Any murder committed with premeditation or ambush is termed assassination.

Art. 3.—Premeditation is the design formed before the deed, of committing an offence against the person of a certain individual, or even of any individual that will be found or met, even were this design to depend on a certain circumstance or condition.

Art. 4—Accomplices of a crime or an offence shall incur the same punishment as the authors of such a crime or offence, except when the law will have disposed otherwise.

Art. 5.—Shall be punished as accomplices of an action termed crime or offence:

Those who by gifts, promises, menaces, abuse of authority or power, culpable machinations or artifice, shall have provoked such an action

Those who shall have procured arms, instruments or any other means employed to commit the action, knowing that they were to be employed to commit it;

Those who knowingly shall have aided or abetted the author or authors of the action, in the facts which led up to, or facilitated or prepared it, or in those that completed it..................

Art. 6.—Those who knowingly shall have received all or part of any things stolen, embezzled or obtained through a crime or an offence shall also be punished as accomplices of such a crime or offence.

Art. 7.—However, when capital punishment shall be applicable to the authors of a crime, it shall be replaced with regard to the receivers, by hard labour for life.

Art. 8.—Whoever shall be guilty of assassination, parricide, infanticide or poisoning shall incur capital punishment.

Art. 9.—Murder shall be punished by death, when it will have preceded, accompanied or followed another crime.

Art. 10.—Whoever has fraudulently taken away a thing which does not belong to him is guilty of theft.

Art. 11.—Whoever shall have voluntarily set fire, to edifices, vessel, boats, stores, woodyards, when they are inhabited or are used for habitation, and generally to places inhabited or used for habitation, whether they belong or do not belong to the author of the crime, shall be punished by death.

Art. 12.—The penalties edicted by the law against the one of those of the accused who will have been deemed guilty, but in whose favour will exist extenuating circumstances, shall be modified as follows :

If the penalty edicted is death, the Court shall apply the penalty of hard labour for life or hard labour for a time. Condemnation to hard labour for a time shall be inflicted for five years at least and twenty years at the most according to the appreciation of the Court.

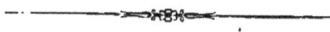

The Mixed Franco-Siamese Court.

AFFAIR OF KHAM MUON (KIENG-CHEK)

SECOND PART.

THE TRIAL.

First Sitting, Monday 4th June, 1894.

SUMMARY.—Preliminary proceedings.—Reading of the art of accusation.—Examination of the Accused.

The sitting is opened at 8 A. M. The Court is composed of M. Moudot, President of the Court of Appeal of Hanoi (President) and four Judges, namely: M. Cammatte, Councillor of the Court of Appeal at Saigon, M. Fuynel, Procureur of the French Republic at Mytho, Phya Maha Amati Thibodi and Phya Kassem Sukari. M. Durwell, Procureur of the Republic at Saigon appears for the prosecution, and M. Duval of Saigon, instructed by M. Tilleke, the Accused's Solicitor, appears for the defence.

M. M. Hardouin and Xavier sit on the bench as interpreters. Also appear as interpreters M. M. Paul Nhu, Nai Yem, Nai Aroun, Khun Borivan.

The President reads the Article of the Convention constituting the Court. He calls for the Accused Phra Yot and demands his name, age and profession. Then the President states the charge upon which the accused is arraigned and explains that the Court is assembled to faithfully, religiously and independently fulfil its duties with strict regard to Justice and equity.

The statement is translated to the accused by M. Xavier. Phra Yot is then accommodated with a seat and the Act of Accusation is read by the Recorder in French, and afterwards in Siamese by an interpreter.

ACT OF ACCUSATION.

The Procureur of the Republic acting as Public Prosecutor in the Mixed Court of Bangkok;

Considering the steps of procedure followed against the accused, Phra Yot Muang Kwang;

Considering Article 3 of the Franco-Siamese Convention of the 3rd October 1893,

Has the honour to state as follows:

About a year ago, during the day of June 5th 1893, the Inspector of Militia, Grosgurin, ordered to escort the Siamese mandarin Phra Yot Muang Kwang from Kham Muon to Outheno, disappeared at Kieng Chek, with the greater part of the Annamite militiamen who composed the small detachment placed under his orders. The circumstances which preceded and lead up to that unfortunate event, and those which accompanied and followed it may be summed up thus:—

For several years now the Laotian provinces of the upper Mekong, situated on the left bank of the river and forming part, from time immemorial, of the Empire of Annam, placed under our protection, had been invaded by the agents of the Siamese Government; amongst the most important of these territories is the province of Kham Kurt, which formed till 1893 the two districts of Kham Cot and Kham Muon, both administered by Annamite mandarins. About that time, Siam, taking advantage of the troubles of the Court of Hué, believed herself strong enough to assume authority, and commenced to establish herself in the region; in fact in 1886 the Siamese mandarin Phra Yot went and officially occupied, in the capacity of Khaluang, the post of Kham Muon.

That irregular proceeding could not fail to arouse the attention of the Government of the French Republic, which lost no time in taking the measures necessary to safeguard the interests of the protected country. This was the situation, when in the month of

May, 1893, M. Resident Luce, of the province of Vinh, received from the Governor-General of Indo-China the order to proceed to Kham Muon, his mission being to occupy that post and again vindicate the full and free exercise of rights which had been so little respected until then. On the 18th May, the French delegate presented himself before the fort, occupied by the Khaluang Phra Yot, to resume possession of the province in the name of his Government; and on the 22nd of the same month, after useless parleying, full of delays and reticence, he decided to take official possession of the fort. At the same time he notified to the Siamese mandarin, whose men had been disarmed to prevent any conflict, that he was going to accompany him to Outheue to assure him a safe protection against the Laotian population of the country who in his administration had animated with feelings rather unfavourable to himself: that unpopularity, which had raised vigorous protestations on the part of Phra Yot, is established by precise and detailed facts. An essentially pacific character, then, must be ascribed to the small detachment placed under the orders of Inspector Grosgurin and composed only of 20 militiamen (linh-co), and a Cambodian interpreter named Boon Chan. Phra Yot, at first, agreed to these decisions and on the evening of the 25th, the eve of the day fixed for his departure, he addressed to M. Resident Luce a letter the real dignity of which it is impossible to contest, but which implied an engagement of honour, which the writer could not break without being guilty of felony. He handed over, in fact, in the terms of that important document, to the care of the Representative of France, the territory of Khammuon and all its dependencies, as well as its officials and inhabitants, making only in the name of His Majesty the King of Siam, his master, the reservations and protestations imposed upon him by his office. He prayed, besides, the Resident to be good enough to transmit his letter to the Governments of France and Siam, that they might fully examine the legal aspects of the question and arrive at a definite solution. Such were the textual terms of that document which constituted a real capitulation, and by which Phra Yot, disclaiming all personal responsibility, formally engaged to take no action on his own authority.

It is in these conditions and under the faith of that treaty, that the small body of Franco-Siamese troops, the one escorting the other, quitted Khammuon on the 26th May. After five days' marching, while good feeling between the two officials and their men did not seem to have ceased, the travellers reached the post of Kieng Chek, situated on the Nam-Hin-Boon, 60 kilometres from Outheue, where they were compelled to wait while the inhabitants got together the boats necessary for transport on the river. M. Grosgurin whom the latter days of forced marching had fatigued, was in a state of weariness and weakness which had forced him to keep to his bed since his arrival at Kieng Chek.

From that moment the attitude and intentions of Phra Yot appear to have changed. He seeks, at first to scatter as much as possible the escort which seems to annoy him, and instead of occupying, with his men, the shelter near the French encampment which M. Grosgurin had informed him he intended as his residence, he takes himself off directly to an abandoned Laotian village, near to Kieng Chek, and settles there. The French officer did not seem to attach much importance to this first incident, but having learned the next day, by his interpreter, that one of the officers of the detachment, named Luang Anurak, was spreading alarming reports in the neighbourhood, and sought to alienate the surrounding population from us by announcing an early offensive return of the Siamese troops, he resolved to put an immediate end to that state of things by securing the person of the impostor. With that intention he had himself conducted to Phra Yot's house, and made that person point out the man he (Grosgurin) sought, and ordered the militiamen who accompanied him to seize him (Luang Anurak). It is wrong to try to attribute, as has been done, to that energetic act an aggressive and hostile character; he acted only with the object of avoiding all motive for a conflict, and to stop, by arresting their author, reports the persistence of which might put an end to the concord which had reigned between the two parties until then. Besides, no direct violence was exercised towards the prisoner, no bad treatment was inflicted upon him, and the assaults he complains of must be attributed to his own resistance. M. Grosgurin limited himself to retaining him in the house he occupied himself, and having him kept under observation, reserving to himself on arrival at Outhene, the right to hand him over to the Siamese authorities.

This arrest, which the circumstances imposed, became a pretext for Phra Yot to still further remove from the neighbourhood of the French detachment: the same day he sent to Inspector Grosgurin a request that Luang Anurak should be set at liberty, and immediately took advantage of a refusal to retire with his party to the rock of Wioug-Krasene, a naturally fortified position situated about five hours from the village of Kieng Chek. It is here that he met, *by chance*, as he has dared to say in his affidavit, the Siamese troops from Outhene, at the head of which he was to march on Kieng Chek. The explanation of that chance is found in a document produced to the Court at the first trial, and the importance of which dominates all this action. Scarcely two days after the departure from Khum Muon, on the 28th May, the accused Phra Yot addressed, to the Siamese authorities at Outhene a pressing appeal the terms of which give an exact impression of his intentions towards the small escort of French soldiers which accompanied him. Without making any allusion to the capitulation he had just signed, he asked in that letter that there should be sent immediately, by forced marches, reinforcements with which he could take the offensive and drive back the French soldiers. This act constitutes a real treason, and is alone sufficient to condemn the one who has committed it. It was on the receipt of that letter that the mandarin of Outhene, Luang Vichit, caused to be sent in the direction of Kieng Chek the two detachments which joined Phra Yot's party at the rock of Wiong Krasene; the instructions written, although not signed, which can be read on the back of the document, and the declaration of the officer Nai Tooi who alludes to having had communication of the document before his departure from Outhene, leave no doubt in that respect.

Thus we arrive at the very day of the outrage.

On the morning of the 5th June, Phra Yot's little troop, re-inforced by the two detachments commanded by Nai Tooi and Nai Plank, took the way to Kieng Chek: one can reckon, even relying on the statements of the Siamese officers, on over 100 armed men composing that little corps; two of Phra Yot's soldiers, previously disarmed at Kham Muon, carrying guns as well. At three o'clock they arrived at Kieng Chek. Almost immediately the fusillade commenced, the fire burnt on all sides, the hut inhabited by M. Grosgurin was not long before it was destroyed, and the unfortunate officer, who had been mortally wounded at the commencement of the attack, perished in the flames; the same fate was reserved to almost all the militiamen who accompanied him, and some only escaped by a miracle. Two of them, the Cambodian interpreter Boon Chan, who has since succumbed from the effects of his wounds, and the militiaman Nguyen Van-Khan, also wounded, have been found. After the massacre and the fire, the aggressors organised a pillage, and everything which had not fallen a prey to the flames, arms and effects which had belonged to the French, were immediately transported in the Siamese junks and became the property of the authors of that too easy victory. The affidavits of the two witnesses who escaped from the massacre are absolutely explicit on this point. Finally I must recall here the odious treatment these two unfortunate victims had to submit to in the course of the long painful journey from Kieng Chek to Bangkok; injuries and humiliations, tortures and menaces of death, they were not spared any of these.

Several versions of the facts which have been briefly touched upon, some of Siamese origin, the others from an Annamite source, have been produced in the course of the inquiry and during the first trial of this affair; but in presence of the contradictions they disclose, and in default of an enquiry on the spot it is as well to accept that which good sense and the concatenation of circumstances indicate, that which the written proofs previously mentioned more precise and clear than the general and very confused evidence, seem to impose. Grosgurin and his militiamen were the victims of a real surprise, a surprise long premeditated, brutally conceived and prepared, and if they, on their side, fired on the Siamese troops, they only acted in legitimate self-defence. The real instigator of all this drama is none other than the accused, Phra Yot. His previous actions, his presence at the moment of the attack, his direct action on the troops placed by him at Kieng Chek, and, at last, the order to fire which he gave, are so many exact facts that his own affidavits establish, and if the accusation has not been able to prove, from lack of immediate inquiry, his direct participation in the assassination of Grosgurin, there are nevertheless laid to his charge the facts of undeniable complicity by aid and assistance, complicity by instructions given, for which complicity he incurs a responsibility even greater than the author of the crime.

It is in vain, therefore, that Phra Yot should seek to invoke for his acquittal a letter which was addressed to him from Nongkhai under the date of 20th May, by Luang Vichit; this document and the instructions it contains are anterior, to the events of Kham Moun, and cannot refer thereto.

It is in vain also that he has pretended, for his defence, that his first intentions, on his arrival at Kieng Chek, were of an absolutely pacific character, that he only came there as an interceder for the liberty of Luang Anurak: it is well-known what was the result of these pretended negotiations, carried on at the head of a veritable small army.

Consequently: The accused Phra Yot Muang Kwang, about 40 years of age, Siamese mandarin, formerly Royal Commissioner at Kham Muon and Kham Kurt, born at Nakon Swan (Siam), residing at Bangkok, is accused:

1. Of having, at Kieng Chek (province of Outhene), on the 5th June 1893, been an accomplice in a wilful homicide committed on the person of the Inspector of Militia, Grosgurin, a French officer attached to the Annamite province of Vinh, in provoking by culpable machinations and artifices, to the said homicide; in giving himself to the author or authors, instructions for its committal; in procuring arms and other means of action, knowing they would be used for that purpose and in aiding and knowingly abetting the authors in the acts which prepared, facilitated, and consummated it.

With this circumstance that the said homicide was committed with premeditation.

2. Of having, under the same circumstances of time and place, and by the same means enumerated above, become accomplice of the crime of wilful homicide committed on the persons of divers Annamite militiamen and of the Cambodian interpreter Boon Chan.

With this circumstance, that the said homicides were committed with premeditation.

3. Of having, under the same circumstances of time and place, been an accomplice in divers thefts of personal property, effects and apparel, arms and munitions, committed to the prejudice of the same and of the Annamite militiaman Nguen van Khau and knowingly concealing all or part of the articles stolen.

With this circumstance, that the said theft's have accompanied and followed the two crimes of homicide above specified.

4. Of having, under the same circumstances of time and place, been an accomplice of the crime of wilful incendiarism of divers Laotian huts used for habitations, in giving instructions for its committal and knowingly aiding and abetting the authors in the acts which prepared, facilitated and consummated it.

All acts constituting the crimes and complicity in crimes provided and punished by the provisions of the Articles of the Penal Law enumerated by the rules of special procedure in the trial.

Given at Bangkok, the 27th May 1894.

Le Procureur,

(signed) GEORGE DURWELL.

The President then asked the Public Prosecutor if he had any questions to ask concerning the evidence to be produced or the witnesses to be heard.

M. Duryell replied asking that certain witnesses should be heard and that the letters written by Phra Yot to Captain Luce on May 25th and to Nai Um on May 28th and the letter by Luang Vichit to Phra Yot on May 20th 1893, should be read.

The Court consented to this course.

The President then proceeded to examine the Accused.

Before putting any questions to Phra Yot, the President reminded him that he was now before a Tribunal of another race, of another religion, but he might feel assured that he was before a Court just, honourable, and ready to do full Justice to him.

The President: You have been for many years Royal Commissioner on behalf of His Majesty the King of Siam, in the province of Kham Muon?

A.—Yes.

Q.—You have governed that district to the best of your ability?

A.—Yes.

• Q.—According to a document written by Capt. Rivière, the inhabitants were not friendly to you, and you made exactions from them?

Accused denied having made any exaction.

Q.—You were in Kham Muon in 1893 when Capt. Luce was ordered to take over that territory as belonging to Annam?

A.—Yes.

Q.—You resisted him several days, but finally you wrote a letter handing over the territory. It was signed Phra Yot Muang Khuang. (The letter was read to the Accused)? The text is as follow: "I, Phra Yot Muang Kwang, Deputy Commissioner of the Districts of Kamkurt and Kham Muon, write this letter, to you the French Commander: I hereby commit to your care the territory of Kamkurt and Kham Muon with the interests therein contained, while making formal declaration of our continued absolute rights over it.

"Since His Royal Highness Prince Prachak Silparkom ordered me to come up to administer the district of Kamkurt and Kham Muon, (territory which touches on the Annamite frontier at the Post called Tar Mooa) I have taken charge of the district and of the sub-officials and the inhabitants of various nationalities in it, in peace, prosperity and justice.

"But after many years had passed, on the 23rd day of May in the year 112 of the Siamese era, you, and four French officers, having under you more than two hundred soldiers, came and plundered my stockade and caused your soldiers to come and surround and seize both myself and my officers and my men, and pushed and thrust us forth by force of arms and drove us out of our stockade and would not permit me to stay and carry out my official duties and look after the interests of my Government, according to the orders of His Most Gracious Majesty, who is my Sovereign.

"You refused to let me stay, and thrust out both me and my officials and my soldiers.

"I now beg to commit to your care the territory, with the sub-officials, the inhabitants and the Siamese interests therein, (while making formal declaration of our continued absolute rights over it) until such time as I shall receive any instructions, whereupon I shall arrange the measures to be taken subsequently.

"And I require you to send this letter to be laid before the Government of France and the Government of Siam, so that the matter may be examined into, and a decision may be arrived at, and that territory may be returned to Siam, which history and tradition have shown to be hers, and to have been administered by her, until now from the beginning.

(Signed), PHRA YOT MUANG KWANG."

Accused acknowledged having written the letter.

Q.—You reserved the right of Siam to the territory leaving the decision to both Governments.

A.—Yes.

Q.—*Provisionally* you evacuated the territory, and you confided formally the territory to Captain Luce, *provisionally* in favour of France?

A.—I felt that I was evicted from Kham Muon by force and I handed over the territory under protest.

Q.—After writing the letter to Capt. Luce you started for Outheno?

A.—Yes.

Q.—You had an escort of 20 Annamites under Inspector Grosgurin?

A.—Yes.

Q.—Seeing that Grosgurin was stricken down by illness and that his party was weaker than yours, did you mean to treacherously attack him and use reprisals against him when you sent this letter of May 28th to Nai Um?—

The letter was then read. The letter is as follows :—

"I, Phra Yot Muang Quang, Deputy Commissioner of Muang Kam Kurt and Muang Kham Muou, send this letter to Nai Roi To Nai Um, Commissioner of Tar Outhene, and inform him that the French with 20 soldiers are coming to take me down to Tar Outhene, and we have reached Ban Phu Muang. Let Commissioner Nai Roi To Um prepare arms and send them up, so that my men may also be fully armed, as the arms belonging to my party have been confiscated by the French. If the French do not listen to my protest, I with my officers and men will join together to resist them. If the French are allowed to bring me down as far as Outhene the French will develope a much more hostile and high-handed attitude and seize the territory belonging to Siam on the Mekong, and thus the honour of the King will be tarnished, and blame will certainly fall upon you and me. I have only about 40 men, but I am resolved to serve His Majesty will all my power. I request you therefore to send me soldiers and men. Let them march by day and night, and if they arrive, the King's enemies will not be able to adopt so high-handed an attitude towards us."

Q.—How did you come to write this letter to Luang Vichit, three days after having professionally handed over the territory to Capt. Luce, speaking of your patriotism, and urging that steps should be taken to drive out the French, especially as you were travelling in the same direction as your letter? At all events Capt. Luce might have expected that you would be sure to keep the peace until the two governments had agreed about the territory. How could you act as you did without committing treason?

M. Ducal, Counsel for the defence, here objected that Phra Yot was unable to follow the Court. He objected to the construction placed upon certain words *i.e.* "handing over."

M. Xavier, interpreter, then repeated the question.

Accused answered that there was a custom in the country that when anyone handed over property under protest, an attachment was made, representing the right to again enter into possession of the property

M. Ducal. Phra Yot strictly followed Siamese law.

Q.—Why did you first hand over the territory under such an attachment, and then write such a letter to Luang Vichit?

A.—I was compelled to write the first letter. I had the feeling that I was evicted by force, but I did not intend, in the letter, to give up the territory.

Q.—Notwithstanding that you had left the territory and that you had written for instruction, did you think you still had power to write for soldiers to come and assist you?

Accused said that under the reservation he made in writing the first letter, he thought he was justified in writing to Luang Vichit.

The President. The Court will note the *valeur morale* of this mental reservation.

Q.—You followed the course of the river Nam Tlin Boun and stopped at Kieng Chek?

A.—Yes.

Q.—Did Grosgurin explain to you why he arrested Luang Anurak?

A.—He told me because Luang Anurak had spread certain alarmings rumours at Kham Muon that the Siamese would return in force.

The President. Grosgurin had a perfect right to arrest Luang Anurak after that, in self defence, for he was in an unknown country and only had a handful of men whose fidelity was doubtful.

Q.—The day after the arrest you left for Vien Krasene where you found reinforcements which had been dispatched in consequence of your letter of may 28th.

Why did you return to Kieng Chek?

A.—To ask for the release of Luang 'Anurak.

Q.—Considering that France and Siam were not at war at the time, why did you take such a large body of men to ask for the release of Luang Anurak, seeing that Grosgurin and the Annamites were living in private houses?

A.—I had not at the time the least intention of attacking Grosgurin. I simply went to ask for the release of Luang Anurak.

Q.—It is quite impossible to believe that Grosgurin who was sick and whose party was the weakest would be first to attack. The Siamese witnesses have stated that there were at least 100 men surrounding the house.

A.—I have already stated there were not more than 50 or 60 men, and the witnesses must have been mistaken.

Q.—Grosgurin was very ill and it is quite incredible that he should have fired upon peaceful men, without any provocation. What can you say to that? according to your own version Grosgurin began the firing.

A,—Grosgurin's party commenced firing and killed Khoon Wang, who was sent up to ask for Luang Anurak's release.

Q.—Supposing they did fire and kill one of your men, you killed 15 of theirs. You say yourself you had 50 men when you left Kham Muon and there were 50 others with Nai Tooi and Nai Plaak. That makes 100.

A.—My men were only 15.

Q.—How can you explain that Boon Chan and the Aunamite soldier, who were examined separately, both give a different version to yours, and say that Grosgurin was sick in bed and the Aunamites were expecting no aggressive action at all? They both state that you came with a numerous troop and that the Siamese commenced firing. It is impossible to suppose that these two witnesses should have agreed together seeing that one was examined at Bangkok and the other else where.

Accused answered he could not help their having told such a story.

Q.—What interest had Boon Chan in saying what he did? You are an influential man in a high position and a poor man like him could have no interest in charging you with such an action; The charge is then that Grosgurin was assassinated in a cowardly manner, that the *attentat* was directed by you, Phra Yot, and that you are the author or accomplice of the crime.

M. Duval. I would ask that the circumstances of Phra Yot's meeting with Nai Toi and Nai Plaak be related; what was agreed upon between them, whether the officers had orders from Vichit and if Phra Yot saw those orders.

Accused answered this question saying : When I met Nai Plaak and Nai Tooi they showed me their orders.

M. Duval. And you sent Koon Wang forward to ask for the release of Luang Anurak?

Accused here stated that after Grosgurin had been told that peace would be broken, Luang Anurak jumped from the verandah when immediately a shot was fired from the house which killed a soldier from Korat. Several other shots followed and two more men fell before the Siamese began firing. The men of Grosgurin were arrayed at the foot of the stairs. Grosgurin was above.

The President. That version is difficult to believe, all the witnesses have agreed that this was not so, in their depositions in Saigon and Bangkok.

The public Prosecutor. Did M. Luce tell the accused the motive of the escort?

A.—No.

The Public Prosecutor. Was the accused in any way troubled during the march?

A.—In leaving Kham Muon wo were between filos of soldiers. Our men were partly Laotians, partly Siamese. After the first shot I shouted: "let us talk, it is not too late."

The President. Did you give the order to fire?

A.—I said, do what you like.

The President here read a report from M. Garauger, made after an enquiry at the spot which read as follows :

The report read as follows :—

On arriving at Kieng Chek, the Inspector took up his quarters at some hundred metres from Phra Yot. Fearing that Phra Yot might play him some trick; M. Grosgurin sent some one to fetch Phra Choun, Phra Yot's subordinate, the next morning that he might keep him near him until a sufficient number of boats were got together to descend to Outhéne. Phra Yot made no observation. Phra Yot came to see the Inspector and told him, in a friendly manner, that he was going down to Thong Lam, to await him there, which is a day's journey on the Nam-Hin. Boun and Phra Yot left immediately with his disarmed men. Three days afterwards he received three hundred Laotians sent by the Governor of Lamabourg and of Outhène, with ten Siamese commanded by Nai Van, come from Nong Kai, at the request of Phra Yot, made on the eve of his departure from Khammoun. On the third day of the moon of the seventh month, towards nine in the morning, the Inspector was sitting on the verandah of the house built on piles, dressed only in his vest and pants, when the sub-lieutenant saw a strong armed band appear before him, while Nai Van and six other Siamese were coming directly towards the house. The Inspector did not seem to understand anything about the arrival of this band, and his interpreter, Boon Chan, had gone to seek victuals at the neighbouring village. In spite of the ten Annamite militiamen who were standing at the foot of the ladder, the seven Siamese were able to come close up; from his verandah the Inspector attempted to carry on a conversation, but without his interpretor it was impossible for him to understand the new comers. He then made a sign to the Siamese to ascend to the verandah. Grosgurin was then standing on the threshold of the door communicating with his bedroom and the verandah, leaning with one hand upon the doorpost. Nai Van then gave the Inspector to understand that he must give up to him Phra Choun, if he did not he would have to take him by force of arms. Grosgurin replied that he would give up Phra Choun as soon as he arrived at Outhene. During this explanation Phra Choun jumped out of one of the openings and ran away. Phra Yot, who during the parleying had caused the house to be surrounded, seeing his subordinate out of danger, cried "fire, fire." The ten militiamen were killed on the spot. The Inspector dropped back, his body being in his bed room. Nai Van himself received a Siamese bullet in his stomach (of which he died). The militiamen had only time to fire three rounds. The interpreter, Boon Chan, on hearing the firing came up at a run, and as soon as he came in sight he received two bullets and was immediately seized.

Did the Laotians fire? Yes, many of them; they were obliged. Phra Yot was among them with his revolver in his hand, threatening to kill those who did not fire.

Phra Yot then set fire to the house, in which the body of Grosgurin lay, and then immediately ordered his men to embark for Tong Lam. He returned three days afterwards to instal himself at Kieng Chek and. at the same time, to inter the remains of the Inspector and Phra Yot's subordinate, Nai Van.

(Signed) GARANGER.

Outhene, 24th May 1894.

One of the Siamese Judges endeavoured to make accused comprehend the purport of this but the extempore translation not being very successful the accused could not reply thereto.

The Court therefore adjourned till 8 o'clock on Tuesday morning.

SUMMARY.—Examination of the witnesses for the Prosecution.

Nyugen Van Khan was the first witness called.

The President.—What is your name, age and profession ?

A.—Nyugen Van Khan, Annamite militiamen.

Q.—You are neither related nor connected to Phra Yot ?

A.—No.

Q.—Raise your right arm and swear to speak the truth and nothing but the truth.

A.—I swear.

Q.—Tell us what you know of the affair of Kieng Chek. You were in the service of M. Grosgurin. Tell us what you have seen.

A.—I went with the accused from Kham Muon to Kieng Chek.

Q.—Give us all the particulars. How many of the killed went from Kham Muon to Kieng Chek ?

A.—I do not remember.

Q.—Tell us what happened there; what you have seen. How many days did you stay at Kieng Chek before the *attentat*.

A.—I was about 10 days at Kieng Chek.

Q.—You do not appear to understand what I ask you. Tell us how long, how many days, you were at Kieng Chek when the *attentat* took place ?

A.—Eight or ten days. I was with four of my comrades in the house of M. rosgurin. I saw a Siamese band arrive who surrounded the house, and fired near the house after which they set fire to the building. I was hidden myself because I was wounded and I saw M. Grosgurin lying dead.

Q.—When you arrived at Kieng Chek where did M. Grosgurin stay ?

A.—In a house.

Q.—On the way from Kham Muon to Kieng Chek were you near M. Grosgurin ?

A.—I was near him, and saw him constantly.

Q.—Was he ill or well ?

A.—He was very ill and was unable to eat.

Q.—And on arriving at Kieng Chek was he better or worse ?

A.—He was very ill on the elephant, and on arriving at Kieng Chek, he could scarcely walk, and immediately went to bed.

Q.—Did you see him often ?

A.—Yes, every day.

Q.—Where was he ? Was he oftener lying down than standing up ?

A.—He was generally lying down, but sometimes got up.

Q.—Do you know anything about the arrest of Luang Anurak ?

A.—Yes.

Q.—Did you see the arrest of Anurak ?

A.—I was in the neighbourhood.

Q.—I ask you if you helped to arrest Luang Auurak ?

A.—No, I did not.

Q.—When Anurak was arrested how was he made a prisoner ? Had he irons on his feet or hands ?

A.—No he was not bound.

Q.—Where was Phra Yot staying at the time ?

A.—Near the house of M. Grosgurin.

Q.—At what distance ? Tell us exactly as you can remember ?

A.—About as far as from here to the other side of the river (which is about 400 yard).

Q.—Just now you were telling us what happened. Go on with your story.

A.—When M. Grosgurin arrived at Kieng Chek he sent the elephants back to Kham Muon as well as the men who had carried the provisions. He was very ill, and had been in bed for 10 days. Phra Yot had many men with him, and one day he came and surrounded the house and fired upon us. It was then about 3 o'clock in the afternoon.

Q.—Who was in the house?

A.—There were five Militiamen and the interpreter.

Q.—Did you see the Siamese around the house? Could you say how many there were?

A.—I saw them but I did not count them. They were all round the house.

Q.—Attend carefully. You say these were five men with M. Grosgurin, but he left Kham Muon with 20. Where were the others?

A.—They were below and around the house.

Q.—When they saw the Siamese, did they form in ranks?

A.—M. Grosgurin called out to them, but they had not time to obey before the firing began.

Q.—What did Anurak do?

A.—He was in the house and jumped out as soon as he saw Phra Yot come.

Q.—Before the Siamese attacked, did no one attempt to parley?

A.—I was not present.

Q.—You do not quite understand the question. Tell us as you can what you have seen? You swear that the first shots were fired by the Siamese?

A.—Yes.

Q.—Were there any persons killed or wounded?

A.—At that particular moment I could not see. I was told afterwards by Boon Chan.

Q.—Did you see Grosgurin die?

A.—No, I saw him when he was dead.

Q.—Did you see him hit, and before he was dead?

A.—No, I was not there, I was hit by the same fire.

Q.—Have you really seen Grosgurin dead?

A.—Yes he was on his bed dead.

Q.—Are you sure of that?

A.—Yes.

Q.—Between the firing and the time you saw M. Grosgurin on his bed, was there time to place him there?

A.—I do not know, I was wounded.

Q.—Look well at the accused. Was he amongst the Siamese soldiers who surrounded the house?

A.—I do not know him well. He has a mark which I do not see.

The Public Prosecutor here remarked that the mark was on the side of the accused's face.

Witness : Yes he was at Kham Muon.

The President. But have you seen him among the men who surrounded the house.

A.—No, I did not see him.

The President here asked the Public Prosecutor if he had any questions to ask the witness.

The Public Prosecutor. Yes, I wish to ask if on the departure from Kham Muon, they had received orders from M. Grosgurin relative to their conduct towards the Laotians and the men they escorted.

The President. Did Grosgurin instruct you what to do, and how to treat Phra Yot? Did he tell you not to illtreat or rob the people?

A.—Yes, we were told to take nothing without paying for it.

Q.—After you were wounded did the Siamese take anything belonging to you?

A.—Yes, my rifle, and everything else.

Q.—Did they illtreat and strike you, specially on the way, and fasten you on board the boat?

A.—No they did not strike me. During the journey they assisted me.

Q.—When you were at Kieng Chek did you see anyone put fire to the house and from what side?

A.—Yes the house was fired on all sides.

The President then asked the Public Prosecutor if he had any further questions to put to the witness. On receiving a reply in the negative, he asked the accused's Counsel if he had any questions to ask the witness.

M. Duval. I should like to ask the witness where were the Annamites exactly stationed at the time of the first shot.

A.—Below the house near the stairs.

M. Duval. Just now he said around the house. He must be exact.

A.—They were near the stairs.

M. Duval. · I wish the Court to note the contradictions of the witness.

A discussion then took place between the President and M. Duval.

Examination continued :

Witness. I was in the house and, at the first shot having been wounded, I jumped down from the house.

The President. Being wounded he fled.

M. Duval. Did he see or did he even hear the shots fired ?

A.—No.

M. Duval. Did he see the firing ?

A.—Yes, but more than once.

M. Duval. Of what nationality were those who fired ?

A.—Siamese.

M. Duval. At what distance were they.

A.—Very near.

M. Duval. You say that no one in the house fired before ?

A.—No one.

M. Duval. But did they fire after ?

A.—I cannot remember, I was wounded.

M. Duval. Did you see any Siamese officers enter the house ?

A.—Yes.

M. Duval. When and who ?

A.—One officer who wore a sash.

M. Duval. Could you say if it was Phra Yot ?

A. I am not sure.

M. Duval. It was after the firing ?

A.—Yes.

M. Duval Just now he said that after the first shots he was wounded and fled.

The Public Prosecutor. The witness was wounded and concealed himself behind a tuft of bamboos from whence he saw all was going on.

M. Duval. After the first firing M. Grosgurin called the guard, did it come ?

A.—Yes immediately ; but the Siamese were then near the house and those who were wounded fled.

M. Duval. How were you able to see the officers enter the house since you had also fled ?

A.—I saw everything from the clump of bamboos where I was concealed.

M. Duval. Was the first gunshot fired before Anurak jumped out of the window ?

A.—At the same moment.

M. Duval called attention to the inconsistency of this answer.

On the question being repeated, witness said the shot was fired immediately afterwards.

The President now insisted, at the request of the Prosecution, on witness saying whether he saw the first firing as well as heard it.

Accused, Yes.

Q.—And was it immediately after Anurak jumped off the house ?

A.—Yes.

Q.—Are you sure that the Siamese fired first ?

A.—Yes—I saw Anurak jump out of the house for I watched him for some distance ; I saw him running in the direction of his friends the Siamese.

Q.—Where was he when the first shot was fired ?

A.—When I saw him, firing was taking place on all sides.

Q.—What distance was Luang Anurak from the house when the first shot was fired?

A.—About as far as the end of this room. Luang Anurak had reached the Siamese when the first gun shot was fired. The Siamese then approached the house and there was a general firing.

The President then asked a Siamese Interpreter if he would repeat to the accused the substance of the examination of the witness. The Interpreter said it was too long, and that it would be necessary to begin again the examination for him to interpret properly.

As the Interpreter of the Legation spoke Siamese as well as French, the President bade him repeat the examination. The translation of the evidence concluded, the President asked if accused had anything to say against the depositions.

Accused said. Nothing.

M. Duval. Asked the President to enquire of the Interpreter if he had carefully repeated the last sentences of the witness to the accused and also to the judges.

The Public Prosecutor asked if the Interpreter had properly translated the statement of witness that the first shots were fired from the Siamese side; and that the escape from the house had preceded the firing.

Accused then asked whether witness was a " boy," or a soldier, and whether he had been wounded. He added that he did not recognise him, and did not remember having seen him.

The President then read a medical certificate certifying to certain wounds received by the witness, and said that witness was a militia man and not a "boy."

One of the Siamese Judges asked if Nguon Van Khan had fired.

A.—No he had not.

Q.—Why?

A.—Because I had not my rifle and I was wounded.

The 2nd Siamese Judge asked whether the house had been set on fire in front or from behind?

A.—I saw the house on fire in front but I do not know what others did as like every one, I thought it best to fly.

The Court at this Juncture adjourned for a few minutes, to consider how to deal with the evidence of Boon Chan, given at the previous trial, Boon Chan having since died.

The President on returning, announced that it had been decided to have the evidence read.

The *Recorder* therefore, read that evidence in French, when the *President* interrupted and asked if the prosecuting and defending Counsels would agree to take French version as read.

This was agreed to on both sides, on the condition that the evidence might be referred to in addressing the Court.

Nai Aroon then read the evidence of Boon Chan in Siamese.

The President asked accused if he had anything to say against the evidence.

Accused said there was much that was not true.

The Court then adjourned at 10.45 until Wednesday morning.

Third Sitting—Wednesday 6th June 1894.

SUMMARY :—Examination of the witnesses for the defence : Luang Anurak.

The Court opened at 8.05 a.m. when the witnesses for the defence were immediately called.

The first witness was Luang Anurak.

After giving his name, age and rank he was sworn.

The President. You were under the orders of Phra Yot ?

A.—Yes, as assistant.

Q.—Tell us what happened at Kham Muon.

Witness began the history of the Kham Muon affair from the beginning, when the President suggested he should go more rapidly, and that he should come to the events that directly referred to the *attentat.*

M. Duval, Counsel for the defence, begged that the depositions should be full and complete as being of great importance, and he had also several questions to put to the witness.

M. Duval then asked what were the sentiments which guided witness and Phra Yot when they wrote the letter to M. Luce and in what spirit they had written that letter, since he (witness) was consulted in the drawing up and forwarding of the letter.

Witness. We agreed together on the form the letter should take, and it was written according to the Siamese custom and contained the protests applicable to such a case.

The President. Let us come to the letter to Nong Kai. Under what conditions was it written ? Do you remember that letter ?

A.—Yes, I am quite aware of the letter referred to. I member it quite well, though not the exact terms. Only generally.

The President. Very good.

M. Duval. I would suggest that witness be examined on the subject of his arrest.

The President. Where and how were you arrested ?

A.—I was arrested at Kieng-Chek. M. Grosgurin, accompanied by Boon Chan and nine or ten men, annamite soldiers, came to see Phra Yot. Phra Yot asked what he wanted, when Grosgurin replied that he would see presently.

Q.—Relate the circumstances of your arrest.

A.—Grosgurin and Boon Chan then spoke together, when Grosgurin asked, " where is he." Phra Yot said " there he is."

Q.—Then they arrested you ?

A.—Grosgurin and Boon Chan again spoke together. I did not know what they said. Then the soldiers seized me by the neck, the shoulders, the arms, and struck me savagely.

Q.—Then they took you to the house of M. Grosgurin ?

A.—They tied my hands and pushed me into a boat, and took me to the house of M. Grosgurin.

Q.—How many days were you with M. Grosgurin ?

A.—Five or six days.

Q.—What happened on the sixth day ?

A.—After five days I heard a great noise. I saw Grosgurin and the soldiers run outside, also Boon Chan. I saw Khoon Wang and Boon Chan near the stairs. Grosgurin was on the verandah and I was near him.

Q.—You then jumped down ?

A.—No, not just then. Khoon Wang said to Boon Chan : " I come with instructions from Luang Vichit to demand the release of Luang Anurak, the handing over of our arms and other property to Phra Yot, and the evacuation of Siamese territory by the French. Boon Chan repeated this to M. Grosgurin who replied " that it was impossible." I was then called by Phra Yot. Boon Chan spoke to Grosgurin who seized me by the hand and cried " Cay, Cay." An Annamite soldier then ran up, came into the house and took a rifle. At this moment Boon Chan ran up, and Grosgurin tried to pull me into the house. Grosgurin was inside though still on the verandah. I saw the " Cay " load the rifle and I broke away and jumped down from the house. At the moment I jumped down I heard a shot from the house.

M. Duval. That is important. The shot was fired as Anurak jumped.

Witness. When I jumped down I heard the shot, and I saw a Korat soldier fall dead. I ran to Phra Yot and asked him what we had better do. Phra Yot said do not fire yet, we must first try to arrange matters. At this time I heard two other shots and turning round I saw Khoon Wang and another soldier fall.

The President. Very good, go on.

Witness. Then Phra Yot, Nai Plaak and Nai Tooi consulted together, Nai Tooi and Nai Plaak wanted to return the fire.

Q.—Are Nai Plaak and Nai Tooi superior, equal, or inferior in rank to Phra Yot?

A.—Phra Yot is a civilian official; the others were military men. I cannot be sure who was superior but I believe Nai Tooi and Nai Plaak were in command of the men.

The President then asked the Public Prosecutor and *M. Duval* if they had any questions to ask witness.

Both having answered in the negative, witness was told to go and sit down. He placed himself behind Phra Yot. As he was turning away, *The President* asked him: during those latter events was Grosgurin ill or well. Did he appear to you strong and vigorous?

A.—He had fever but he could walk.

The second witness for the defence, Nai Tooi, was then called, and sworn.

The President. Do you hold and inferior rank to Phra Yot?

A.—I am a Captain.

M. Duval. As Nai Tooi was under the orders of Luang Vichit before quitting Kham Muon, and had received orders and instructions from Vichit to find Phra Yot, it would be well if he gave details on these points.

The President. On quitting Outhene you received orders to go where?

M. Duval. Were his orders written or verbal?

The President. What orders did you receive? Were they written or verbal?

A.—I received written orders first and afterwards verbal orders.

Q.—From whom?

M. Duval here complained that the translation was not properly rendered and that the replies of witness were not accurately conveyed to the President.

The President was understood to say that M. M. Hardouin and Xavier were there to control any fault of interpretation and that their competence in this respect was undoubted.

The President. After you had received orders what did you do?

A.—I received orders to deliver Phra Yot and to make the French evacuate the territory.

Q.—Where did you come from?

A.—From Outhene to Wieng Krasene.

Q.—How many men had you?

A.—About 50 or 60.

Q.—How many men were there under other officers at Wieng Krasene?

A.—There were only nine and those of Phra Yot.

Q.—How many had Phra Yot?

A.—About 19 or 20.

Q.—There were altogether then about 90?

A.—Only about 60.

Q.—You went to Kieng Chek the day after your arrival?

A.—Yes.

Q.—What did you do?

A.—At Kieng Chek Phra Yot sent Khoon Wang to demand the release of Anurak.

Q.—It was then Phra Yot who gave that order?

A.—Yes, after the three of us (Nai Plaak, Phra Yot and myself) had consulted together.

The President said that the Court would accept the version placed before the Siamese Court of the arrest of Anurak, if the defence had no objection.

M. Duval. Ask the witness what orders they (the three) gave after their Conference, apropos of the orders received from Outhene.

The witness was recalled and the question put by the President.

Witness. At Wieng Krasone I communicated to Phra Yot the orders of Vichit, ordering us to demand the freedom of Phra Yot, and the evacuation of the territory by the French. But as Phra Yot was free and Anurak a prisoner, it was necessary to go and deliver the latter.

M. Duval. Had you orders to deliver him by force?

A.—No, we had no orders to deliver him by force.

Q.—You were then at Kieng Chok with fifty rifles when you saw Anurak jump from the house?

A.—Yes.

Q.—Did you hear any shots?

A.—Yes, the first one.

Q.—Any others afterwards?

A.—Yes.

Q.—From the Siamese?

A.—At the first shot a Korat soldier fell; then after two or three other shots came from the house we asked to parley with the French, but they continued to fire. We then replied.

Q.—The witness said that beside setting Phra Yot free, they had orders to make the French evacuate the territory. Has this been properly translated?

A.—Yes.

The Public Prosecutor asked if Luang Vichit had really shown him the letter on the back of which he had written the orders?

M. Duval said that that was agreed to by the defence.

The President. The letter has been produced by you?

A.—Yes.

Khoon Narong, the next witness was then called and sworn.

Q.—You were with Phra Yot when Anurak jumped down?

A.—Yes. When Anurak jumped out of the window one shot was heard.

Q.—Did you see Anurak arrested?

A.—Yes.

Q.—How many days was he with Grosgurin?

A.—Four or five.

Q.—Did you see him jump to the ground?

A.—Yes.

Q.—Did you hear the shots at this time?

A.—Yes.

Q.—Where were you?

A.—At the foot of the stairs.

Q.—What were you doing there?

A.—Nothing.

Q.—Were you armed?

A.—I had a rifle.

The President (sharply). He was doing nothing. He was walking about with a rifle in company with 50 or 60 other armed men like himself at 3 o'clock in the afternoon.

Q.—How did you come there?

A.—I was with Khoon Wang who had come to demand the liberty of Anurak.

The President. Then he was doing something. When one comes with 80 armed men around a house, one comes for something.

Q.—Tell us what you saw?

A.—I was with 4 or 5 soldiers of Phra Yot and 50 men of Nai Tooi who had come to demand the release of Anurak and the evacuation of the territory.

Q.—After the first shot did you hear others?

A.—Anurak jumped down, then there was one shot; then others which killed Khoon Wang. I heard the officers and Phra Yot tell the men not to fire.

M. Duval. The order to fire was given after the first shot?

A.—The Siamese replied by firing a number of shots.

The President. Nai Tooi had 60 men; how many had Nai Plank with him?

A.—The two troops numbered about 50 to 60 men.

The Public Prosecutor. Were the troops Laotians or Siamese?

A.—Siamese.

The next witness Honin visot, a soldier, was called and sworn.

The President. He does not appear very intelligent.

M. Duval requested that his deposition should be taken.

Q.—Were you present at Kieng Chek and did you see Anurak jump down?

A.—Yes.

Q.—Did you see Grosgurin?

A.—No I did not see him.

Q.—After the first shot, you heard others?

A.—Two other shots were fired after the one when Anurak came out.

Q.—Then, nothing more, all was finished?

A.—I heard other shots again and heard Phra Yot call out to wait.

Q.—Where was Phra Yot?

A.—In front of the house.

Q.—Had he a rifle?

A.—No a sword.

The Public Prosecutor. Of what nationality is the witness?

A.—Siamese.

Khoon Chamnung was then called and sworn.

Being asked by the President to lift up his right hand to take the oath, witness, evidently unaccustomed to this European way of proceeding laughed.

The President commented severely upon the attitude of the witness.

The President. You are the man who took two bottles of medecine from the house of M. Grosgurin?

A.—No.

Q.—You were, however, recognised by Boon Chau as having taken those flasks of medecine?

A.—It was not I.

Q.—Did you see Anurak jump down?

A.—Yes.

Q.—A shot was then fired?

A.—Yes.

Q.—Who fired it?

A.—Some one in the house.

Q.—Were there other shots?

A.—Yes, others which killed Khoon Wang.

Q.—Did you see anything else?

A.—I do not remember anything else very well.

The Public Prosecutor asked the nationality of witness.

A.—Siamese.

Khoon Vichit a Siamese in the service of Phra Yot, the next witness was called and sworn.

Q.—Were you at Kieng Chek with Phra Yot?

A.—Yes.

Q.—Did you see Anurak jump from the house?

A.—Yes.

Q.—At this moment a shot was heard ?

A.—Yes.

Q.—Whence came it ?

A.—From the house.

Q.—Were there other shots ?

A.—Anurak ran towards us and then there were other shots.

The President. Was this witness examined before the first Court ?

A.—No, he did not give evidence before the other Court.

The President then called Nai Plaak, the next witness.

M. *Duval* produced a certificate from Dr. Deuntzer stating that Nai Plaak was ill and unable to attend Court. This certificate was read in French and in Siamese.

This concluded the evidence.

The Court then adjourned for five minutes, after which the Public Prosecutor delivered his speech for the Prosecution.

The Public Prosecutor first called the attention of the Court to the disputes which had of old existed between the Empires of Annam and Siam about the sovereignty of the left bank of the Mekong. He gave a historical sketch, from a French point of view, of the origin of the recent differences between France and Siam concerning the same territory. The provinces of Kham Kurt and Kham Muon both situated on the borders of the Laotian country and of Annam proper, were more especially contended for by both neighbouring powers. During recent years Siam tried to consolidate her occupation and to extend it more and more. However, as recently as 1883 we still find that Annamite mandarins were appointed in the name of Annam to rule over Kham Muon and Kham Kurt. But at this time Phra Yot was sent by the Siamese Government as Deputy Commissioner to administer these places and to erect a fort at Kham Muon where we find him still acting in the same capacity in 1893. How he understood his administration, and what his conduct was towards the natives whom he was supposed to protect, we already know from the report of Captain Luce to whom, when he was on his way to Kham Muon, the natives came from all sides complaining of ill treatment and acts of prevarication and of cruelty which they had experienced from the accused. The Counsel for the Prosecution here read an extract from M. Luce's report, stating that the information of M. Luce was strongly corroborated by a Conference held in July last, by a French officer named Rosiere, at the French Geographical Society. This explorer, relating his journey in Laos, speaks very unfavourably of the accused and of the many unpopular acts which he heard had been committed by him as Commissioner of Kham Muon. Monsieur Durrwell quoted two or three instances and especially one where Phra Yot, having to resist a revolt of some of his own men, received a wound the trace of which was still visible on his forehead. In May 1893, the French Government having decided to reoccupy this territory, Captain Luce was sent to Kham Muon in order to take possession of it. This mission was essentially pacific. He had to avoid as much as possible any act of violence; any effusion of blood. He communicated the object of his mission to Phra Yot, who at first showed some intention of resistance, but afterwards changed his mind and consented to leave his post and evacuate the territory. Accordingly, he and his men left the stockade, and the day after the 23rd May, Phra Yot wrote to Captain Luce the letter which had already been read in Court and the importance of which would not have escaped the attention of the audience. The learned counsel then read an extract of this letter in which it is specially said :

"I beg to commit to your care the territory with the sub-officials, the inhabitants and the Siamese interests therein, while making a formal declaration of our continued absolute rights over it, until such time as I shall receive any instructions, whereupon I shall arrange the measures to be taken subsequently, and I require you to send this letter to be laid before the Governments of France and of Siam, so that the matter may be examined into, and a decision may be arrived at, and that territory may be returned to Siam, which maps, history and tradition have shown to be hers, and to have been administered by her until now from the beginning."

Counsel for the Prosecution considered this letter equivalent to a formal agreement, or rather to a capitulation by which the accused distinctly bound himself not to again take up arms against France or to enter into any acts of hostility against her, but to wait until matters should be peacefully settled between the two Governments. Phra Yot had tried by mental reservation or, as the learned Counsel for the Prosecution termed it, by a capitulation of his own conscience, to elude the consequences of this promise. But these consequences were clear, notwithstanding two objections which might, it was presumed, be made on behalf of the defence: First, that Phra Yot simply complied, when he wrote this letter, with a formality very usual in Siamese law and custom, namely, that when anyone is evicted by violence from what he considers to be his legal property, he enters a protest involving an attachment on the object of which he is deprived; Secondly, that he declared in the letter that his future conduct would depend on further instructions. In reply to these objections, Counsel for the Prosecution contended on the first point that the only consequence of this alleged Siamese legal proceeding could be a mutual obligation for both parties to peacefully wait for a decision of the competent authorities, and, on the second point, that Phra Yot himself, without waiting for instructions, had, on the 20th May, sent a letter to Nai Um, in which, reporting the events of Kham Muon, he made no mention of his letter to Captain Luce, but tried to excite his countrymen to acts of reprisal. Captain Luce had decided to send Phra Yot and his party to Outhene, and to furnish an escort sufficient to protect the accused from the eventual consequences of his unpopularity among the natives. Nothing seemed to disturb the good harmony between the parties on the way from Kham Muon to Kieng Chek. They marched without any definite order and not at all as though the Siamese were the prisoners of the French. Only one day before they arrived, Monsieur Grosgurin with his party were in front, and Phra Yot and his party, being left behind to march by themselves, seized the opportunity to lag behind, so that while Grosgurin and his men camped at a place called the New Shelter, Phra Yot and his followers stopped at the Old Shelter, about three hundred yards further down the river. A short time afterwards Monsieur Grosgurin appears to have been informed that a lieutenant of Phra Yot, named Luang Anurak, was spreading a rumour among the natives that the Siamese would come back in force to fight the French and reconquer their lost position. The whole population was alarmed and Grosgurin considered that, as a guarantee for his own security he had to act energetically. On the following day, therefore, he went to Phra Yot's quarters with his interpreter, Boon Chau, and nine or ten of his soldiers, and proceeded to arrest Luang Anurak in the manner that had been related by several witnesses. They were compelled to use violence, but this was justified because Luang Anurak resisted. They opposed violence to violence. On the same evening, Phra Yot sent a messenger to Grosgurin to request the release of Luang Anurak. The request was refused, and Phra Yot could hardly expect anything else, because it could not be presumed that Monsieur Grosgurin would easily have departed from a measure that had been adopted for his own security. Phra Yot took this as a pretext for moving some three hundred yards down the river to a place called Wieng Krasene where he felt secure. There he met, not casually, but as a consequence of his own letter of the 28th May to Nai Um, two officers, Nai Tooi and Nai Plank, who had been sent by Luang Vichit, the Siamese Commissioner, at Outhene, with troops to release him from supposed captivity. The orders of Luang Vichit were written on the back of the above mentioned letter of the 28th May. Circumstances being altered these two officers and Phra Yot consulted together and agreed that Luang Anurak had to be rescued. They decided also to exact from Monsieur Grosgurin the delivery of the goods presumed to have been taken at Kham Muon, and the evacuation of the Siamese territory. In 'execution of this plan they went to Kieng Chek with a force which, if all the evidence were taken into account, might be reckoned at about a hundred men whereof sixty at least were armed with guns. This force was first met by Boon Chau, the Cambodian interpreter, who asked what their intentions were. They said that they wanted the delivery of Luang Anurak and that they intended to ask for it peacefully. Peacefully with sixty armed soldiers! They then went on and stopped at a short distance from Monsieur Grosgurin's quarters. One of them Khoon Wang went to notify what they required from him. Here there are two contradictory versions, what we may call the Siamese and the Annamite versions. The Siamese version is that, during the interview with Koon Wang, Luang Anurak stood next to Monsieur Grosgurin at the top of the ladder that was in front of the verandah. When Monsieur Grosgurin had distinctly refused to comply with Khoon Wang's request, one of the Siamese, probably Phra Yot, called to him to come down, Monsieur Grosgurin took hold of Khoon Wang's wrist and tried to drag him inside the house, calling, at the same time, an Annamite sergeant to come upstairs. The sergeant ascended, took a gun and loaded it, and then Luang Anurak succeeded in wrenching himself free from Monsieur Grosgurin and jumping down from the house. Immediately afterwards a shot was fired from inside the house and a Korat soldier fell dead. Two or three gunshots from the Annamites followed. Two more Siamese soldiers were hit and, after a short consultation between the three Siamese chiefs, it was decided to return the fire. This version thus leaves the whole responsibility of the attack on the Annamites.

The Annamite version is quite different. It is distinctly said that after Luang Anurak had escaped, the Siamese fired first, that Monsieur Grosgurin, very unfortunately, but probably owing to his evident state of illness, omitted to take even the most elementary precautions necessary for future contingencies, that there were not more than five Annamite soldiers in the house, and that the fatal result was the killing of Monsieur Grosgurin himself and of nearly all his soldiers.

The choice between these two versions could not be doubtful. It was certainly to be regretted that M. Luce himself had not had an immediate enquiry made on the spot. This would have greatly facilitated the elucidation of the whole truth. But if the Siamese witnesses who gave their evidence, either before the Siamese Court or before the present audience, were compared with the witnesses for the prosecution, it could not escape attention that the former were taken exclusively from among the Siamese and not the Laotian followers of Phra Yot, notwithstanding it had been abundantly proved that a great part of his followers consisted of Laotians. Then these witnesses had every facility for communicating with one another and there was every likelihood of their being influenced by their chief, living and being examined, as they were, all in the same place. Boon Chan and the Annamite soldier, on the contrary, were examined quite separately. Boon Chan, who had unfortunately since died, had given his evidence successively before the Siamese authorities, before M. Pavie, Minister of France, and before the Siamese Court, whilst the second was examined first at Saigon by M. Ducos, and afterwards before that Court. They could not thus be suspected of having concocted their depositions together. Moreover, there was a document quite recently put before the Court, namely the report of M. Garanger, the French Commercial Agent in the Province of Outhene, which gave the current version of the event as admitted in the very place where it occurred, and from which it resulted that the responsibility of the agression was to be imputed exclusively to the Siamese chiefs. Although this statement could not be admitted as legal evidence, the information which it gave had undoubtedly a great importance.

For all these reasons Phra Yot was accused of having been, if not the principal author, at least an accomplice in the perpetration of the crimes mentioned in the Act of Accusation.

The Court adjourned at about 10.30.

Fourth Sitting—Thursday 7th June, 1894.

SUMMARY :—Address of M. Duval, Counsel for the Defence.

Messieurs de la Cour.

In one of his most charming fables, the fable in which he shows us a peasant of the Danube laying before the Roman Senate the claims of his fellow citizens, our great poet Lafontaine puts in the mouth of this messenger the three following lines :

" Je supplie avant tout les Dieux de m'assister,

" Veuillent les Immortels conducteurs de ma langue,

" Que je ne dise rien qui doive être repris." (1)

Such is exactly my state of mind as I rise to defend my client ; for I feel the diffi‑, culties of my task, the difficulties of the task of a French lawyer defending a Siamese mandarin who is accused of the awful crimes the Public Prosecutor has related to you.

I beseech therefore the Court, should I fail to conquer one of these difficulties, to be persuaded that my words will have failed to carry the exact meaning of my thoughts and that I shall be the first to regret the lapsus I may have committed.

Considering the gravity of the accusation, the defence must not expose itself to the reproach of having neglected even one of the circumstances alluded to by the accusation, and therefore I shall resume before you the Act of Accusation itself, I shall follow it word by word and shall endeavour to prove to the Court by the documents of the case, and by the contradictions of the witnesses for the Prosecution and by the evidence of the witnesses for the defence that Phra Yot is innocent of the crime which he is accused of.

The Act of Accusation begins thus :

" For several years now, the Laotian provinces of the upper Mekong, situated on the " left bank of the river and forming part, from time immemorial, of the Empire of An- " nam, placed under our protection, had been invaded by the agents of the Siamese Gov- " ernment ; amongst the most important of these territories are the province of Kham Kurt, " which formed till 1893 the two districts of Kham Cot and Kham Muon, both adminis- " tered by Annamite mandarins. About that time, Siam, taking advantage of the troubles " of the Court of Hué, believed herself strong enough to assume authority, and commenced " to establish herself in the region ; in fact in 1886 the Siamese Mandarin Phra Yot went " and officially occupied, in the capacity of Khaluang, the post of Kham Muon.

" That irregular proceeding could not fail to arouse the attention of the Government " of the French Republic, which lost no time in taking the measures necessary to safeguard " the interests of the protected country. This was the situation when in the month of " May, 1893, M. Resident Luce, of the province of Vinh, received from the Governor " General of Indo-China the order to proceed to Kham Muon, his mission being to occupy " that post and again vindicate the full and free exercise of rights which had been so little " respected until then."

Allow me to dwell a few minutes on these first words of the accusation. I do not believe, gentlemen, that I have to follow the accusation on this ground. It little matters, to my mind, in this affair, to whom belonged, at the time of the Kham Muon events, the left bank of the Mekong, or whether the respective claims of the French and Siamese Governments were founded or not, I have to defend Phra Yot against a well defined accusation, and I have only to consider the matter as regards what specially concerns Phra Yot.

For the last eight years, the fact is acknowledged by the Prosecutor himself, my client, occupied the post of Kham Muon, according to the orders of the King of Siam, his master ; never, for eight years, had he been disturbed in this occupation ; he had therefore the right to consider himself the lawful master of the region, and had he not considered himself so, he only had to obey the orders which com- pelled him to remain there. He had not to take any part in political opinions and dis- cussions ; he was a governor intended to govern and not to discuss the acts of his, superiors.

(1) I must begin by beseeching the gods to assist me. May the Immortals guide my tongue so that I say nothing that may deserve to be blamed.

Let us now resume the Act of Accusation.

"On the 18th May the French delegate presented himself before the fort, occupied "by the Khaluang Phra Yot, to resume possession of the province in the name of his "Government; and on the 22nd of the same month, after useless parleying, full of delays "and reticence, he decided to take official possession of the fort."

Here, gentlemen, let me give my opinion on the conduct of the accused. The Act of Accusation does not say that at that moment accused did not oppose the least resistance, that he acted as a coward, that he surrendered the place which his duty obliged him to defend. But accused will have to account for such conduct to his superiors, and the consequences may be very serious for him, but this is of little moment for the present.

I now come to the letter written by Phra Yot to M. Luce:

"At 'the same time M. Luce notified to the Siamese mandarin, whose men had been "disarmed to prevent any conflict, that he was going to accompany him to Outhene "to assure him a safe protection against the Laotian population of the country whom "his administration had animated with feelings rather unfavourable to himself: that "unpopularity, which had raised vigorous protestations on the part of Phra "Yot, is established by precise and detailed facts. An essentially pacific character, "then, must be ascribed to the small detachment placed under the orders of "Inspector Grosgurin and composed only of 20 militiamen (linh-co), and a "Cambodian interpreter named Boon Chan. Phra Yot, first, agreed to these "decisions and on the evening of the 25th, the eve of the day fixed for his departure, "he addressed to M. Resident Luce a letter the real dignity of which it is impossible "to contest, but which implied an engagement of honour which the writer could "not break without being guilty of felony. He handed over in fact, in the "terms of that important document, to the care of the Representative of France, the "territory of Kham Muon and all its dependencies, as well as its officials and inhabitants, "making only, in the name of His Majesty the King of Siam, his master, the reservations "and protestations imposed upon him by his office. He prayed, besides, the Resident to be "good enough to transmit his letter to the Governments of France and Siam, that they "might fully examine the legal aspects of the question and arrive at a definitive solution. "Such were the textual terms of that document which constituted a veritable capitulation "and by which Phra Yot, disclaiming all personal responsibility, formally engaged to take, "no action on his own authority."

Notwithstanding the reserve which I have laid to myself as a rule, gentlemen, it is impossible for me not to say here a few words concerning the way in which M. Luce's march on Kham Muon must be appreciated.

As I have already endeavoured to prove to the Court, Phra Yot had the absolute right to consider himself the lawful Governor of the province. Thus, when M. Luce presented himself before Phra Yot's post, and ordered him to abandon it, it is impossible to admit that the latter could have considered this otherwise than as a violation of Siamese rights, as contrary to the orders which he held from his chiefs, in one word, as an act of hostility. Oh, I know, gentlemen, that Phra Yot's conduct in this matter is far from being exempt of blame, I do not wish to ask you, gentlemen, by what word you would characterise the conduct of one of our officers who would abandon, without the least resistance, the post which France would have confided to his care. I consider that Phra Yot's responsibility towards his Government is very heavy and I should not care to have to justify his conduct in this respect.

Phra Yot committed an act of cowardice which he fully realised the next day, once the first feeling of fright had passed away; and then it was that he wrote to M. Luce that letter the importance of which rules the whole of this case, that letter on which, you, Monsieur le Procureur de la République, base the whole of your accusation and of which I shall make the basis of my defence.

These are the words used by Phra Yot, according to the translation accepted by the Court:

"I, Phra Yot Muang Kwang, Deputy Commissioner of the Districts of Kamkurt and Kham Muon, write this letter, to you the French Commander: I hereby commit to your care the territory of Kamkurt and Kham Muon with the interests therein contained, while making formal declaration of our continued absolute rights over it.

"Since His Royal Highness Prince Prachak Silparkhom ordered me to come up to administer the district of Kamkurt and Kham Muon, (territory which touches on the Annamite frontier at the Post called Tar Moon) I have taken charge of the district and of the sub-officials and the inhabitants of various nationalities in it, in peace, prosperity and justice.

"But after many years had passed, on the 23rd day of May in the year 112 of the Siamese era, you, and four French officers, having under you more than two hundred soldiers, came and plundered my stockade and caused your soldiers to come and surround and seize both myself and my officers and my men, and pushed and thrust us forth by force of arms and drove us out of our stockade, and would not permit me to stay and carry out my official duties and look after the interests of my Government, according to the orders of His Most Gracious Majesty, who is my Sovereign.

"You refused to let me stay, and thrust out both me and my officials and my soldiers.

"I now beg to commit to your care the territory, with the sub-officials, the inhabitants and the Siamese interests therein, (while making formal declaration of our continued absolute rights over it) until such time as I shall receive any instructions, whereupon I shall arrange the measures to be taken subsequently.

"And I require you to send this letter to be laid before the Government of France and the Government of Siam, so that the matter may be examined into, and a decision may be arrived at, and that territory may be returned to Siam, which history and tradition have shown to be hers, and to have been administered by her, until now from the beginning.

(Signed), PHRA YOT MUANG KWANG."

Here, gentlemen, we have to examine a point of Siamese law which has, indeed, an equivalent in our own law. Several times during the course of these debates I have requested, Monsieur le Président, to ask the witnesses what was the exact meaning of the Siamese word which the interpreter has translated by "I confide to your care." The witnesses' answers proved that there exists an old Siamese custom by virtue of which when in a distant region where no Court and no official exist, two people disagree on the right of ownership to a thing, one of them *Confides* the thing to the other and goes and lays his claim before the nearest Court or official. Phra Yot feeling incapable of defending Kham Muon confided it to M. Luce and very honestly warned him that he did so reserving all his rights, and that he was going to apply to his superiors for orders; this is undoubtedly the meaning of this sentence "until orders will have "reached me after which I shall take further measures."

It has never entered the mind of Phra Yot, as the accusation has it, to surrender his territory to France definitely and to accept the acts of M. Luce: he had not the right to do so. This letter is very clear and may be condensed in the following words: *I yield to strength being incapable and not desiring to take upon myself to resist, but as soon as I shall have received orders I shall obey them.*

And with perfect logic and consistency, two days after he applies for these orders to Nai Roi, his chief, in the following letter:

"I, Phra Yot Muang Kwang, Deputy Commissioner of Muang Kam Kurt and Muang Kham Muon, send this letter to Nai Roi To Nai Um, Commissioner of Tar Outhene, and inform him that the French with 20 soldiers are coming to take me down to Tar Outhene, and we have reached Ban Pha Muang. Let Commissioner Nai Roi To Um prepare arms and send them up, so that my men may also be fully armed, as the arms belonging to my party have been confiscated by the French. If the French do not listen to my protest, I with my officers and men will join together to resist them. If the French are allowed to bring me down as far as Outhene the French will develope a much more hostile and high-handed attitude and seize the territory belonging to Siam on the Mekong, and thus the honour of the King will be tarnished, and blame will certainly fall upon you and me. I have only about 40 men, but I am resolved to serve His Majesty with all my power. I request you therefore to send me soldiers and men. Let them march by day and night, and if they arrive, the King's enemies will not be able to adopt so high-handed an attitude towards us."

This letter carried by a messenger arrives at Outheue where Luang Vichit comes across it; it is opened by the superior officer who immediately puts two of his officers Nai Tooi and Nai Plaak at the head of sixty men and sends them to Phra Yot with the following written orders:

" Let Nai Tooi march forward as fast as possible; wherever Annamite soldiers shall " be met, let them be driven back; if they resist they must be fought, let your men "strongly settle at Kieng Check. Whatever happens, deliver Phra-Yot so as to have " thus the assistance of his men."

These orders and these reinforcements reach Phra Yot at Kieng Chek. (I have passed under silence so far M. Grosgurin's march for nothing important happened to call attention to it).

What was then the respective situation of both sides?

M. Grosgurin seeing Phra Yot's attitude, and hearing the rumours that circulated amongst the inhabitants, had reflected that he had perhaps acted rather light'y and tried to find a means of hitting a decisive blow.

Phra Yot's lieutenant, Luang Anurak, provided him with an opportunity ; he spread rumours of resistance which reached M. Grosgurin's ears.

The latter then accompanied by the interpreter Boon Chan and several armed Annamite soldiers came to the old shelter where Phra Yot had camped and required that Luang Anurak should be delivered up to him; notwithstanding Phra Yot's refusal Anurak was seized, ill treated, bound and carried off manu militari to the house where Mr. Grosgurin lived.

It is after this arrest that Luang Vichit's men arrived at Kieng Chek. Phra Yot informed the two lieutenants of the situation, and all three decided that to obey their orders they had to require Grosgurin to give up Luang Anurak, and should they meet with a refusal, to obtain his release by force.

Phra Yot's secretary, Khoon Wang, was sent to parley, and he did not hide to M. Grosgurin that to keep Anurak a prisoner any longer would be breaking the treaty made between the two companies.

M. Grosgurin refused and Khoon Wang come and reported the result of his interview to Phra Yot. The latter, considering this refusal, and together with Nai Tooi and Nai Plaak decided to go to Grosgurin with all their men and make another application.

They, thus, marched towards the house and again parleyed with M. Grosgurin who persisted in his refusal, and Phra Yot, considering that Luang Anurak was unjustly maintained a prisoner, called the latter. Luang Anurak came on the verandah and was violently pushed back inside the house by M. Grosgurin himself; he then managed to escape, jump from the verandah and join his companions.

These facts, gentlemen, are undoubtedly proved by the evidence you have heard ; the witnesses for the prosecution themselves do not give the prosecution the means of not holding these facts as absolutely correct.

We now come to the principal circumstance of this case : to the murder, says the accusation ; to the battle, says the defence.

The Act of Accusation on this important point is wonderfully concise : "Nearly at the same time, the firing began, and fire was lit on all sides."

Well, let us examine, whether the witnesses for the prosecution, gave Monsieur l'Avocat Général the right to hold this sentence as correct, whether the witnesses for the defence do not destroy it completely, and do not prove the diametrically opposite version.

The first witness, the most important undoubtedly, who seems to corroborate the Act of Accusation is the Cambodian interpreter Boon Chan. Let us see how he relates the principal scene.

In the statement written in his own hand, and delivered to H. R. H. Prince Prachak, Boon Chan declares " that at that time (i.e. at the time when Luang Anurak escaped) I heard the firing of guns. Unfortunately I do not know who began to fire first."

In the statement of 20th October, 1893, before M. Pavie, he declares " *I cried to our Militia-men : to arms! and I went out to prevent the Siamese from firing, but they would not listen to my request and began at a distance of 5 or 6 metres firing on the house.*"

Before the Siamese Court the same Boon Chan states as follows: " *Grosgurin then rose and told me to enquire what all these warlike preparations meant. I explained: Do not fire, do not fire, let us have an explanation first. They began to shout fire but they had not yet fired.*"

Such is, gentlemen, the evidence on which is built this capital Accusation : a witness who tells you first *I do not know who began to fire first*, who later on says *that the Siamese began to fire first* and who finally declares that the same Siamese *had not yet fired*, can such a witness be worthy of confidence, and in your inmost conscience is it possible for you to form any opinion whatever from these three different versions ? How could so important a circumstance as the first firing have escaped the notice of Boon Chan who from his own admission stood on the verandah next to Grosgurin at the critical moment? How could one, in the presence of these three different versions not be of opinion at the very least that such an evidence must be put aside?

But this is not all, the second witness, the link-co Ug-van-Khan is not more decisive.

To Monsieur le Resident Ducos, on the 15th December 1893, he replied that at the moment when the Siamese fired, he was on guard at the foot of the ladder of the house occupied by M. Grosgurin.

In Court, he contradicted himself. I have already at the time requested the Court to make a note of it, and said on the contrary that he was with three of his companions in the upper part of the house.

Moreover, in the statement he made to the Court two days ago I request the Court to note an undeniable improbability : Ug-van-Khan pretended he had been wounded amongst the very first, pretended that he had gone down from the upper part of the house, that he had taken refuge under the stairs of the verandah ; that then from there he had reached the clump of bamboo where the Siamese found him.

Wounded, indeed, how could the witness be stupid enough to expose himself to more blows in leaving the interior of the house and hiding under those stairs where he could not reach without having gone down the said stairs and consequently without having exposed himself as a target to the Siamese shots.

Much more extraordinary still is that imprudent flight he pretends to have made from under the stairs where supposing he had doubled himself up he might have been safe, to that clump of bamboos which he could not reach without crossing a piece of ground swept by the shots.

All this is unlikely, inadmissible and the Court certainly will value it for what it is worth.

As a natural consequence, I am now led to compare with this fragile evidence that of the witnesses for the defence.

Here the witnesses' attitude is different and is not, as Monsieur le President seemed to insinuate in the course of these debates that of witnesses repeating a lesson learnt by heart, but of witnesses stating the truth : if these men have all come and made the same statement to the Court it is because they told the truth, the unadulterated truth.

All these witnesses, gentlemen, without one exception, stated that the first firing came from the house, at the moment when Luang Anurak escaped, that Khoon Wang had been hit by it and had died, consequently that two other Annamite shots had killed two Korat soldiers, and that it was only after having undergone these three firings that Nai Tooi, Nai Plaak and Phra Yot, of one accord, had given order to fire in return.

The evidence before the Siamese Court of Nai Tooi who was unable to appear before you has been read and has corroborated these facts : Phra Yot's statement was identical.

Let us even, gentlemen, consider the situation leaving aside the witnesses. There is one fact proved, acknowledged by the Annamite linh-co himself, that is that firing began, just at the very moment when Luang Anurak jumped from the verandah. Well, is it likely, is it possible to admit that the Siamese would have fired on the house as Luang Anurak was crossing the space which separated them from the house. They would infallibly have killed him. I insist on this point, gentlemen, as I have already done in the course of these debates. Ug Van Khan was very plain : it is just at the moment when Luang Anurak escaped that the first shot was fired. Mousieur le President asked him to measure the distance that separated the two groups at that moment : it was proved that this distance was 20 metres. Well, Luang Anurak would never have had time to cross that space of 20 metres, and would have fallen under the shots of his own soldiers.

The true version, the version which the evidence and which sound logic corroborate, gentlemen, is that one of the Annamite soldiers who had charge of Luang Anurak fired at the prisoner who was escaping, that his shot killed Khoou Waug, that two of his companions fired immediately after him, killed two Siamese, and that it is only then, in order not to allow themselves to be massacred without resistance, and in an absolute case of legitimate self-defence that the Siamese men answered the firing and caused the unfortunate results which we now deplore.

I believe, gentlemen, I have made this point sufficiently evident, and I can without dwelling any longer upon it, come to the last sentence of the Act of Accusation :

"It is in vain, says he, that Phra Yot should try to find an excuse for his conduct "in a letter addressed to him from Nong-Khay on the 20th May by Luang Vichit : this "document and the instructions it contains are anterior to the events of Kham Mœr and "cannot apply to them."

The defence has never meant to plead that this letter could have reached accused Phra Yot before the events of Kieng Chek. I only wish to argue from it to show that it was in the Siamese intentions to resist the French by force of arms and that orders were given in that sense.

There is the letter : it does not need to be commented upon :

Nongkhai, May 20th 1893.

"I am instructed by H. R. H. Prince Prachak Silparkhom, the Royal Commissioner "of Lao Puen, to acquaint you that a report of Phya Suriyadet has been received, in "which it states that Luang Mol Yothamyog reports as follows :

"On the 5th May 1893 at about 3 o'clock in the afternoon, Ong-Ram-thu the French "Governor of Puseen (Annam), another Ong-Kamthu the French Commander, Quan-ba "a French officer and a Frenchman whose name were unknown to Luang Mol, came "to Topone with 400 soldiers, and arrived at Luang Mol's camp at Chieng Rom. At the "time Luang Mol was sick with fever and confined to his bed, his officer cried out that "the French force arrived at the camp, when Luang Mol came out of his room, the French "force signalled by their bugle for their soldiers to force into the stockade and then the "French officer ordered their men to surround Luang Mol, who reports that if he desired "to escape he could then have been able to do so, but he saw at the same time that he "could not successfully resist the French and he resolved to remain at his post to "sacrifice his life for His Majesty's service without attempting to retreat or escape. "The French then kept him as a prisoner in another house and intended to take him to "Phine and to the Mekong.

"Furthermore, Luang Vichit and Thow Chiang Choomi made a statement that the French had taken Luang Mol as a prisoner, and took him down to Waug-Khan, and also that they had turned out all our guard from Pha-bang.

"We have therefore prepared our force to march on immediately. Let you, Phra "Yot take good care of every post and road with all your force and prepare to defend "them. *If the French would advance upon you in any manner let you defend against them to "your utmost* I will come at once with soldiers and force from Nongkhai to stay at "Outhone and be ready to assist you as emergency required."

(Sealed and Signed) LUANG VICHIT SARESART.

I repeat to the Court that this letter does not need any comment. It is the evident proof that resistance against French occupation was decided by the Siamese Government ; this is the only point I wished to prove by it.

This letter leads me quite naturally to mention the one which is not mentioned in the Act of Accusation but which Monsieur le President has read at the last sitting. I allude to the letter of M. Garanger.

The version it relates, gentlemen, brings us to the very first version which was spread immediately after the event, according to which Phra Yot would have assassinated M. Grosgurin whilst the latter was lying sick in his bed, with his own revolver torn from his belt.

I need not point out to the Court that M. Garanger is a new comer in the country, that he accepted blindly what may have been reported to him, and that his protégés in order to gain his sympathy had but one object which was to depict Grosgurin as a martyr and Phra Yot as an assassin. I believe, gentlemen, I have successively considered the points and documents which are the most important in this case: I still have to consider the four charges made against the accused and to see which of them you may consider as well founded.

Phra Yot is accused :

"1—Of having, at Kieng Chek (province of Outhene) on the 5th of June, 1893, "rendered himself accomplice of an act of wilful homicide committed on the person of "Inspector Grosgurin, French officer and inspector of militiamen, attached to the pro-"vince of Vinh, by provoking by culpable machinations and artifices the above "monkulted homicide; by giving to the author or authors of it instructions to commit "the murder; by procuring arms and other means of action, knowing for what purpose "they were to be used; and by aiding and abetting, knowingly, the author or authors, "in the acts which prepared, facilitated and consummated the murder."

"With the circumstance that the aforesaid murder has been committed with pre-"meditation."

I believe I have proved that there was no wilful homicide, that the interpretation of the letters compels to put aside all culpable machination, that the instructions were only given in a case of legitimate self-defence, and that the arms were brought by the men of Luang Vichit.

"2—Of having, in the same circumstances of time and place, and by the means "enumerated above, rendered himself accomplice of the wilful homicide committed on the "persons of certain Annamite soldiers and of the Cambodian Interpreter Boon Chan.

"With the circumstance that the aforesaid murder has been committed with premeditation."

The answer to this is the same as the one made to the first charge.

"3—Of having, in the same circumstance of time and place, rendered himself "accomplice of certain fraudulent thefts of personal property, arms and ammunitions, "committed to the prejudice of the same, as well as the Annamite soldier Nguyen Van "Khan, by concealing knowingly all or part of the stolen property. With this "circumstance that the above mentioned thefts have been accompanied and followed by "the two crimes of homicide above specified."

This charge, not having been alluded to in the course of the debates, Nguyen Van Khan himself not having mentioned it in his evidence, and Monsieur l'Avocat Général not having insisted on it, must be put aside by the Court.

"4—Of having, in the same circumstances of time and place, rendered himself accomplice of the crime of arson of certain Laotian buildings, place serving as habitation, by giving instructions to commit the arson, and by assisting knowingly the authors in the circumstances which have led to it, facilitated and consummated it."

It has appeared from the debates that the fact of houses and other property being set on fire was the natural result of the firing. This charge shall also be put aside by the Court. .

Well, gentlemen, seeing that the four charges are thus annihilated, what shall be your verdict ?

According to the rules of proceeding your answer will have to be yes or no.

If you say yes, gentlemen, it will be that I shall have badly fulfilled my task, that I shall not have succeeded to convey to your minds the conviction which has guided me throughout these debates, conviction without which I would not have accepted to defend Phra Yot, and he and I shall respectfully accept your verdict.

If your sentence is no, gentlemen, it will be that you will not have forgotten that this left bank of the Mekong, the region where these unfortunate events have taken place, is to-day French territory, that you will have wished to prove to our new subjects that French Justice is great and impartial, and that it can appreciate according to what they are worth even events which it deplores most.

My task is over, gentlemen. It is with confidence that I trust Phra Yot's fate in your hands.

Luang Chamnong, one of the interpreters, having translated the substance of M. Duval's speech to the Siamese judges,

The Public Prosecutor then briefly replied, contending that the evidence of Boon Chau and the Annamite soldier was more reliable than that of the witnesses for the defence; inasmuch as the latter told a story agreeing at all points, while the former showed some discrepancies. If Boon Chau's depositions were unsatisfactory it must be remembered that they were obtained from him whilst he was a wounded prisoner under fear of death. He further submitted that Phra Yot pledged himself not to do anything till he received instructions from his Royal Master, and that he broke his pledge two days afterwards and attacked his friendly escort.

The President then read to the accused an indictment of twelve counts, chiefly founded on the Act of Accusation and asked him what plea he had to make to each one.

Accused replied that he was not guilty of the accusations laid to his charge, as he left Kham Muon under compulsion. At Kieng Chek he only acted in self-defence and he had throughout obeyed the orders of his superiors.

The President then adjourned the Court till Saturday, 9th June, when he said judgment would be pronounced.

Fifth Sitting—Saturday 9th June 1894.

SUMMARY :—Non-appearance of the Accused.—Judgment put off to a further Sitting.

The Bench took their seats at 4.15 P. M.

The President declared the Court resumed and ordered the accused to be produced, and an official left for this purpose. There was a delay of a few minutes, when the President ordered the Cambodian Interpreter of the French Consulate to see that the accused was brought in.

A few minutes after he came back and stated that the accused was not there.

The President then said :

" The Court, considering that the accused Phra Yot does not appear, and that no "justification of his absence has reached the Court, orders that the case shall be con-"tinued at a further sitting."

The Court then rose.

Franco-Siamese Mixed Court.

AFFAIR OF KHAM MUON (KIENG CHEK).

THIRD PART.

JUDGMENT.

Sixth Sitting—Wednesday 13th June 1894.

SUMMARY :—Reading of the Judgment.

On Tuesday 12th June it was announced that the Mixed Court would assemble the next day at 4 p.m. to deliver Judgment.

At 4.5 p.m. on Wednesday 13th June the Court assembled and the President, after having ordered that the accused should be produced, and the latter having appeared, read the following Judgment:

The Mixed Court which was instituted by and meets in virtue of Article III. of the Convention of October 3rd, 1893, between the Government of H. S. M. the King of Siam and the French Republic, and composed as follows :

    President : Monsieur MONNOT,
        President of the Court of Appeal of Hanoi.
    Members : Monsieur CAMATTE,
        Counsellor of the Court of Appeal of Saigon, Judge.
        Monsieur FUYNEL,
        Procureur de la République at Mytho, Judge.
        PHYA MAHA AMAT THIBODI, Judge.
        PHRA KASSEM SU KARI, Judge.
    Public Prosecutor : Monsieur DURWELL,
        Procureur de la République à Saigon.
    Recorder : Monsieur DE COULGEANS,
    Interpreters duly sworn for the case:
        Messrs. HARDOUIN, French Consul ;
        XAVIER,
        PAUL NHU,
        NAI YEM,
        NAI DROUN,
        KHUN BORIVAN,

gave the following Judgment :—

Whereas in view of the written documents which have been produced, and according to the debates that have taken place during the sittings of the 4th, 5th, 6th, and 7th instant, the facts submitted to the knowledge of the Court may and must sum up as follows :—

The Siamese Mandarin Phra Yot Muang Kwang, for several years occupied, as the King's Commissioner, the region which is bounded by the frontier of Annam, when, about the middle of the month of May 1893, Capt. Luce, French Resident, conveyed to him an order to evacuate the province of Kham Muon, which appeared to have always been comprised within the territory of the Empire of Annam. After having for several days offered a certain amount of resistance to the injunctions of the Representatives of the Republic, he made submission, on May 23rd, by a letter in which he confided the administration of the Province to the care of Capt. Luce, until the Siamese and French

Governments should have decided to whom the territory in dispute belonged. Although that cession was provisional and dependent as to its ulterior effects, on the negotiations which would take place between the Government of H. M. the King of Siam and that of the French Republic, Phra Yot formally pledged himself to accept, until further order, the substitution of French authority, and, consequently, to abstain from all hostile action against the Representative of France. Confiding in the sincerity of that promise, which was of such a nature as to assure him of his perfect security, the Inspector of the Garde Civile, Grosgurin, appointed by Capt. Luce, did not hesitate to undertake, with 20 men only, in a region which he did not know, to accompany the Siamese troops to the frontier. After several days' marching in the direction of Kieng Chek, Phra Yot secretly wrote, and furtively sent, to Capt. Nai, at Outhene, a letter in which, making a strong and pressing appeal to the patriotism of the soldier, he begged and strongly insisted on his quickly despatching arms, men and subsidies of all kinds with a view to a violent and decisive attack against the French.

By this document dated May 28th Phra Yot repudiated the formal engagement contained in the letter he had written five days before to Capt. Luce ; in breaking thus the compact which he had freely made with the French officials without even being able to pretend now that he had received at that moment any order, any advice which led to that sudden determination he not only committed a disloyal act, he spontaneously and voluntarily assumed the penal responsibility of the crimes which would necessarily result as the immediate consequence of that provocation.

Continuing their way towards the Siamese frontier the two small bodies of troops soon reached Kieng Chek, the place designated for a long halt. They had scarcely arrived in that locality when Grosgurin was informed that Luang Anurak, Phra Yot's lieutenant, was trying to stir up trouble against the French. Completely isolated in the heart of a fanatical population, in an almost savage region, and with only a handful of 20 men to protect him, the Representative of France had a right to look to his own security, a right which became a duty having regard to the Annamites placed under his orders. In these conditions he did not hesitate to make sure of the person of Anurak in order to put him out of position of doing any harm; he thus used a right of preventive legitimate defence, which he appears to have exercised with moderation, if one believes the statements of Boon Chan and of Nguyen Van Khan.

The next day, Phra Yot, who had been careful to remove to a certain distance from Grosgurin's house, in order to escape his surveillance, went secretly to Wieng Krasene, five hours' navigation from Kieng Chek, towards Outhene. Two days afterwards he returned bringing forces which had been sent to that place as the result of his letter of May 28th. It is these troops, numbering in the opinion of all the witnesses, 70 men effectively armed, who, on June 3rd, suddenly surrounded the house where Grosgurin was and massacred the Representative of France and the greater part of the Annamites who accompanied him.

The "act of war" not being able to be invoked, since peace reigned between France and Siam—which is expressly recognised by the two Governments in the Convention of Oct. 3rd, 1893, according to which the act specially submitted this day to the examination and Judgment of the Court is termed *attentat*—the criminality of that investment and of the homicides which followed cannot be contested, even if the version given by the accused and supported by some of his companions in arms were admitted. In fact, according to them, Luang Anurak would have run out of the house with the object of escaping ; an Annamite would have fired upon him at the moment, and inflicted a mortal wound on one Korat soldier ; and this act of violence would have immediately provoked the reprisals of the Siamese. If the law allows the legalisation of an act committed when we are menaced with death, it is only in the case in which the imperious necessity of self-preservation makes it a duty. One can only resist an aggression ; and it is evident that Grosgurin, confined to his room by illness, as is attested by all the witnesses who were near him, surrounded by a small number of Annamites, could not for an instant have thought of attacking the numerous armed troops which surrounded his house.

The truth is clearly shown from the respective situations of the Siamese and Laotians on one side, and of Grosgurin with only some Annamites on the other.

If we dismiss the secondary details on which unavoidable contradictions have arisen, the depositions of Boou Chan and Nguyen Van Khan, taken at different times and places (which dispells all suspicion of previous collusion between them) inspire the Court with sufficient confidence to be used as basis to a verdict. The arrest of Luang Anurak, which was a just and legal act, as has been proved, served as a protext for a crime directed against the Representative of France. Under cover of parleying towards obtaining the liberty of Luang Anurak, a band of armed men assembled around Grosgurin's dwelling in a most menacing manner. Whatever may be the point from which the first shot was fired, it is manifest that a violent aggression was prepared and carried out by those who invested and then invaded the house, and that Grosgurin succumbed, without possible defense, to a homicide long premeditated, and carried out in a cowardly manner.

The participation of Phra Yot in this crime is just obvious. It was he who caused troops to arrive, who went himself to fetch them at Wieng Krasene, and who conducted them to the place where, under his direction and with his assistance, they committed the murder which it is the duty of the Court to punish.

The complicity of Phra Yot in the pillage and burning of the house is not shown with the same certainty. It is not impossible, in fact, that these crimes coming after the wilful homicide already mentioned, were accomplished without the knowledge of the accused by one of those minor subalterns, whose uncultivated and savage nature the Court has been able to appreciate.

Considering the application of the penalty :

Whereas, if the acts of which Phra Yot has been guilty present all the characteristics of crimes against common law, the motive which animated the accused, the end he had in view, make an appreciable difference between him and the ordinary assassin who takes away the life of a fellow creature with a view to gratify his cupidity and to satisfy a feeling of hatred or personal vengeance. These divers degrees of moral responsibility must be taken into consideration by a Court of Justice, and ought to correspond with the divers degrees of criminal responsibility; it is through extenuating circumstances that the Judge must equitably determine the exact proportions.

On these grounds the Court has resolved to return the following answers to the questions put to it :—

1st Question.—Has a wilful homicide been committed at Kieng Chek (province of Oathene) on June 5th 1893, on the person of M. Grosgurin, Inspector of Militia of the province of Vinh ?

> Answer : Yes, by a majority.

2nd Question.—Has the said homicide been committed with premeditation ?

Answer : Yes, by a majority.

3rd Question.—Is the accused guilty of having been an accomplice in the crime of homicide above specified and qualified, in provoking by machinations and guilty artifices, in giving himself to its authors instructions to commit it, in procuring arms and other means of action, knowing that they would be used for that purpose, and in aiding and abetting with knowledge its authors in the acts which led up to, facilitated, and consummated it ?

Answer : Yes, by a majority.

4th Question.—Have wilful homicides been committed under the same circumstances of time and place on the persons of 15 Annamite militiamen, not named ?

Answer : Yes, by a majority.

5th Question.—Have the said homicides been committed with premeditation ?

Answer : Yes, by a majority.

6th Question.—Is the accused guilty of having made himself by the same means an accomplice in the homicides above specified and described ? .

Answer : Yes, by a majority.

7th Question.—Have fraudulent abstractions of *objets mobiliers*, effects and clothings, arms and ammunition been committed under the same circumstances of time and place, to the prejudice of the same, as deposed by the Cambodian interpreter Boou Chau, and the Annamite militiaman Nguyen Van Khan ?

Answer : Yes, by a majority.

8th Question.—Did the said fraudulent abstractions accompany, precede, or follow the crimes of homicide above specified ?

Answer : Yes, by a majority.

9th Question—Is the accused guilty of having been an accomplice in the said fraudulent abstractions and of giving instructions to commit them, and knowingly keeping back any part of the objects stolen ?

Answer : No, by a majority.

10th Question—Was the crime of wilful burning of various Laotian huts, places inhabited and serving as habitations, committed under the same circumstances of time and place ?

Answer : Yes, by a majority.

11th Question—Is the accused guilty of having been an accomplice in the said crime of wilful incendiary in giving instructions for its committal and in knowingly aiding and abetting its authors in the acts which led up to, facilitated and consummated it ?

Answer . No, by a majority.

12th Question—Are there extenuating circumstances in favour of the accused ?

Answer : Yes, by a majority.

Mondot, President ;

Camatte, Judge ;

Fuynel, Judge.

Messrs. Phya Maha Amat Thibodi and Phra Kassen Su Kari, Siamese Judges, declared that they refused to sign.

The Interpreters :

Signed : Mondot, President   Hardouin,

Camatte,   Xavier.

Fuynel.

Consequently

The Court, considering articles 1, 2, 4, 5, 8, 9 and 12 of the Special Rules thus worded :

Article 1.—Homicide committed voluntarily is qualified murder.

Article 2.—Any murder committed with premeditation or through ambush is qualified assassination.

Article 3.—The accomplice of a crime or of an offence shall incur the same penalty as the authors themselves of such a crime or offence, except in the case where the law disposes otherwise.

Article 5.—Shall be punished as accomplices of an action qualified crime or offence, those who by gift, promises, menaces, abuse of authority or of power, culpable machinations or artifice, shall have provoked this action or given instructions to commit it ;—those who shall have procured arms, instruments, or any other means employed to commit the action, knowing that they would be employed to commit it ;—those who knowingly, will have aided or abetted the authors of the action, in the facts which led up to or facilitated or prepared it ; without prejudice etc.

Article 8.—Whoever shall be guilty of assassination, parricide, infanticide, or poisoning shall incur capital punishment, etc.

Article 9.—Murder shall be punished by death when it will have preceded, accompanied or followed another crime.

Article 12.—The penalties edicted by the law against the one or those of the accused who will have been deemed guilty but in whose favour will exist extenuating circumstances, shall be modified as follows :

If the penalty edicted is death, the Court shall apply the penalty of hard labour for life or hard labour for a time. Condemnation to hard labour for a time shall be inflicted for five years at least and twenty years at the most according to the appreciation of the Court."

Has condemned and condemns Phra Yot to the punishment of 20 years hard labour; condemns him besides to defray the costs of the trial;

Orders that the execution of the Judgment shall be supervised by the Minister Resident of France in Bangkok.

This Judgment was given in the Hall of the French Legation in Bangkok, the Wednesday thirteenth of June, 1894, at 4 P.M. in a public sitting.

Signed : PAUL MONDOT, President.

CAMATTE, Judge.

FUYNEL, Judge.

HARDOUIN, Interpreter.

XAVIER, ditto.

DE COULGEANS, Recorder.

CONTENTS.

www.ingramcontent.com/pod-product-compliance
Lightning Source LLC
Chambersburg PA
CBHW021601270326
41931CB00009B/1325